Backstage Pass

Written by Sharon Parsons

Contents	Page
Chapter 1. *A Show To Remember*	4
Chapter 2. *Don't Miss Out!*	6
Chapter 3. *The Best Seat In The House*	8
Chapter 4. *Spotlight On The Stars*	10
Chapter 5. *Maximum Impact!*	14
Chapter 6. *Setting Up The Stage*	20
Chapter 7. *The Big Night*	24
Chapter 8. *The Show Rolls On*	30
Index And Bookweb Links	32
Glossary	Inside Back Cover

Backstage Pass

Chapter Snapshots ...

1. A Show To Remember
How many people and how much hard work does it take to stage a performance?

2. Don't Miss Out!
Your favorite group wouldn't even be on stage if it wasn't for all the people working behind the scenes.

3. The Best Seat In The House
To get the best seat in the house, you have to buy a ticket first!

"Let's clip o

4. Spotlight On The Stars

To put on an exciting show, the lighting must be perfect!

5. Maximum Impact!

The sound crew works hard to ensure that the group's words, music, and special effects all reach the audience clearly.

6. Setting Up The Stage

The lighting and sound is perfect, but the stage still needs to be set up.

7. The Big Night

The audience waits excitedly for the lights to dim and the show to start.

8. The Show Rolls On

The audience goes home, but for the group and the crew, the show must go on.

backstage pass and take a look behind the scenes of a concert."

1. A Show To Remember

Have you ever been to a live performance, such as a musical show or a play? If so, you probably recall the bright lights, the entertaining performers, and the excited audience.

How many hours, days, weeks, or months did it take to prepare for the show, before it was ready for you to enjoy?

The First Drama Performances

The first known drama performances took place in ancient Egypt more than 5,000 years ago. The first real theaters were built in ancient Greece about 2,500 years ago.

Behind the scenes, there are many people working to make the stage look spectacular, and helping the performers look and sound their best.

> **What Is A Backstage Pass?**
> A "backstage pass" is a special ticket that allows you to go behind the stage of a concert. Usually, only people who are working on the show get a backstage pass.

Let's grab a backstage pass and take a look behind the scenes of a concert.

2. Don't Miss Out!

Think about how excited you would be if you discovered that your favorite music group was going to perform at a concert in your area.

What Do Advertisements Cost?

Advertisements can be very expensive. A small ad in a newspaper might cost $250. A whole page in a newspaper

Q: What is an advertising company?

When a concert for a famous group is planned, an advertising company lets you and all the group's fans know about the concert beforehand. They want to sell *all* the concert tickets!

The advertising company sends press releases to radio and television stations, newspapers and magazines. Press releases contain information about the band and the dates and locations of their concerts.

They also provide facts about the band that might interest the media's listeners, viewers, or readers.

If a band is very famous, TV shows play their music videos and interview band members. Music stores also advertise the band by setting up big displays of its CDs and posters. They hope to sell thousands of CDs before and after the concert.

CDs

CDs, or compact discs, can store a large amount of information. A CD is made of a light metal called aluminum and has a thin plastic coating on it. A CD player uses a laser beam to pick up information from the CD.

3. The Best Seat In The House

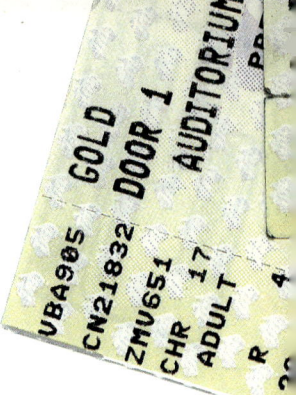

The concert organizers need to print the tickets. Sometimes, for the very famous bands, they will print special tickets with holograms or fancy designs on them. By doing this, people can't copy the tickets and attend the concert for free.

There are three ways that people can buy concert tickets. One way is to phone a ticket company and buy tickets using a credit card.

What's A Credit Card?
A credit card is a plastic card with your name and a special number on it. You can use it to buy things. The bank will tell you how much all the things you bought cost, and then you have to pay it back.

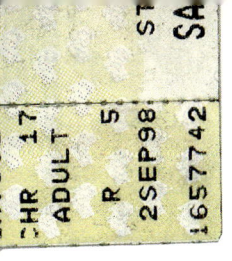

Ano[ther] order t[...] they c[an...] compa[ny...] plan. [...] people [...] to buy [...]

what is a fax machin?

Sor[...] ensive. It all depends on how famous the band is. Also, tickets for very popular concerts sell out quickly, so people have to buy their tickets quickly.

> **Fax Machines**
>
> A fax machine is a machine that uses a telephone line to send a picture of a piece of paper to another fax machine.

> **How Many Seats?**
>
> Some concerts are held in small halls where there might only be room for less than 100 people. Some concerts, by very famous bands, are held in sports stadiums where 100,000 people may turn up!

4. Spotlight On The Stars

The concert organizers want to make the concert look as exciting and colorful as possible for the audience. Hundreds of lights in different colors and shapes make the stage look spectacular. Before the show, the people in the lighting crew plan where all the lights will be positioned.

Scared of heights? If you are, you might not want to work as part of the lighting crew! They have to work high above the stage to place lights on huge beams.

A lighting crew working high above the stage before a big concert.

Often, each light has a little motor attached to it. The lighting crew can move the lights by operating a big, computerized control panel called a console. From the console, they can control where all the lights are pointing, and which lights are on or off.

Special effects lighting is used to create a unique show. Strobe lights are bright lights that flash on and off very quickly. Laser lights flash different-colored lines of light that can be moved around and around. Spotlights beam down on particular performers as they move around the stage.

Lasers
Lasers are very powerful, thin beams of light that can be sent out in straight lines from a special machine.

Ordinary light

Sometimes, special colored pieces of glass or plastic, called filters, are placed in front of the lights. The lighting crew can change the color of the light by changing the filter they use. The lighting crew usually sets up the lights well before the day of the concert so that they can make sure that all the lights work. There must be no problems during the show!

The Color Of Light

Light can be split up into different colors. Ordinary light has seven main colors that we can see in it. They are red, orange, yellow, green, blue, indigo, and violet. These are the colors that we can see in a rainbow. A rainbow is made when tiny drops of water in the air split up light into its different colors.

Red
Orange
Yellow
Green
Blue
Indigo
Violet

5. Maximum Impact!

The sound crew is also backstage, working carefully to make sure the music sounds perfect. They look for the best places to set up the speakers and other sound equipment.

The sound of someone's voice or musical instrument is often not loud enough for everyone to hear clearly in a huge concert hall or outdoor stadium. The sounds that they make need to be made louder, or amplified.

Amplifiers

Sound from a voice can be changed into electrical energy using a microphone. A microphone sends electrical energy along wires to an amplifier. An amplifier increases the amount of electrical energy and sends the increased amount of energy along wires to speakers. The speakers use the electrical energy to vibrate and produce a much louder sound than the original voice.

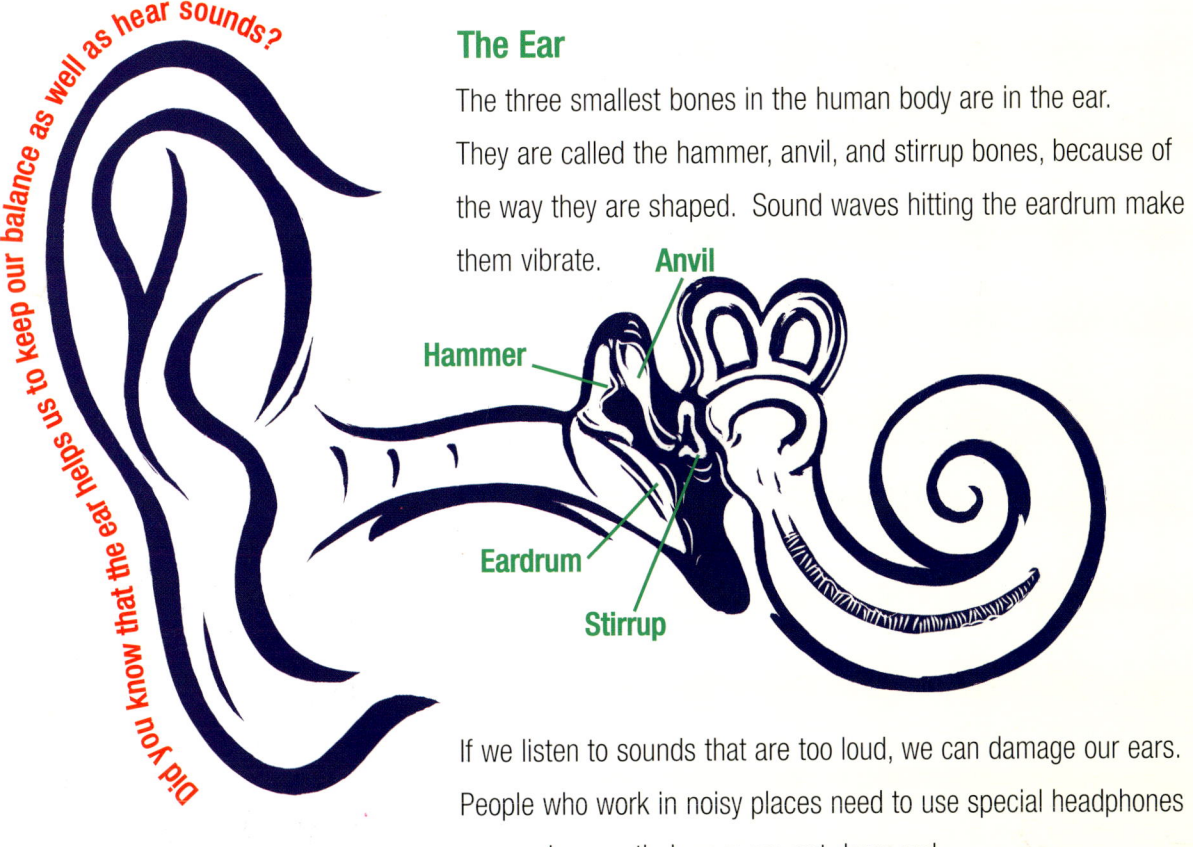

Did you know that the ear helps us to keep our balance as well as hear sounds?

The Ear

The three smallest bones in the human body are in the ear. They are called the hammer, anvil, and stirrup bones, because of the way they are shaped. Sound waves hitting the eardrum make them vibrate.

- Anvil
- Hammer
- Eardrum
- Stirrup

If we listen to sounds that are too loud, we can damage our ears. People who work in noisy places need to use special headphones or ear plugs so their ears are not damaged.

What Is Sound?

Sound is made up of thousands of tiny vibrations. These vibrations travel through the air. Our ears are specially designed to pick up these vibrations, and our brains recognize them as sounds.

The sound crew sets up microphones and amplifiers that the musical instruments are plugged into.

Microphones work by turning sound into electricity. In an amplifier, this electricity is then made hundreds or thousands of times stronger and is then sent to speakers. The speakers use magnets to turn the electricity back into sound again—but the sound is much stronger and louder than the original sound.

Technology in music allows musicians to create special sound effects. This can make a guitar or a piano sound loud and exciting, or soft and low. Sound-effects technology can be used to make one voice sound like two or three voices all at once, or to create an echo.

Even though opera singers are trained to sing loudly, opera singers, such as Luciano Pavarotti, use microphones so that everyone will be able to hear them!

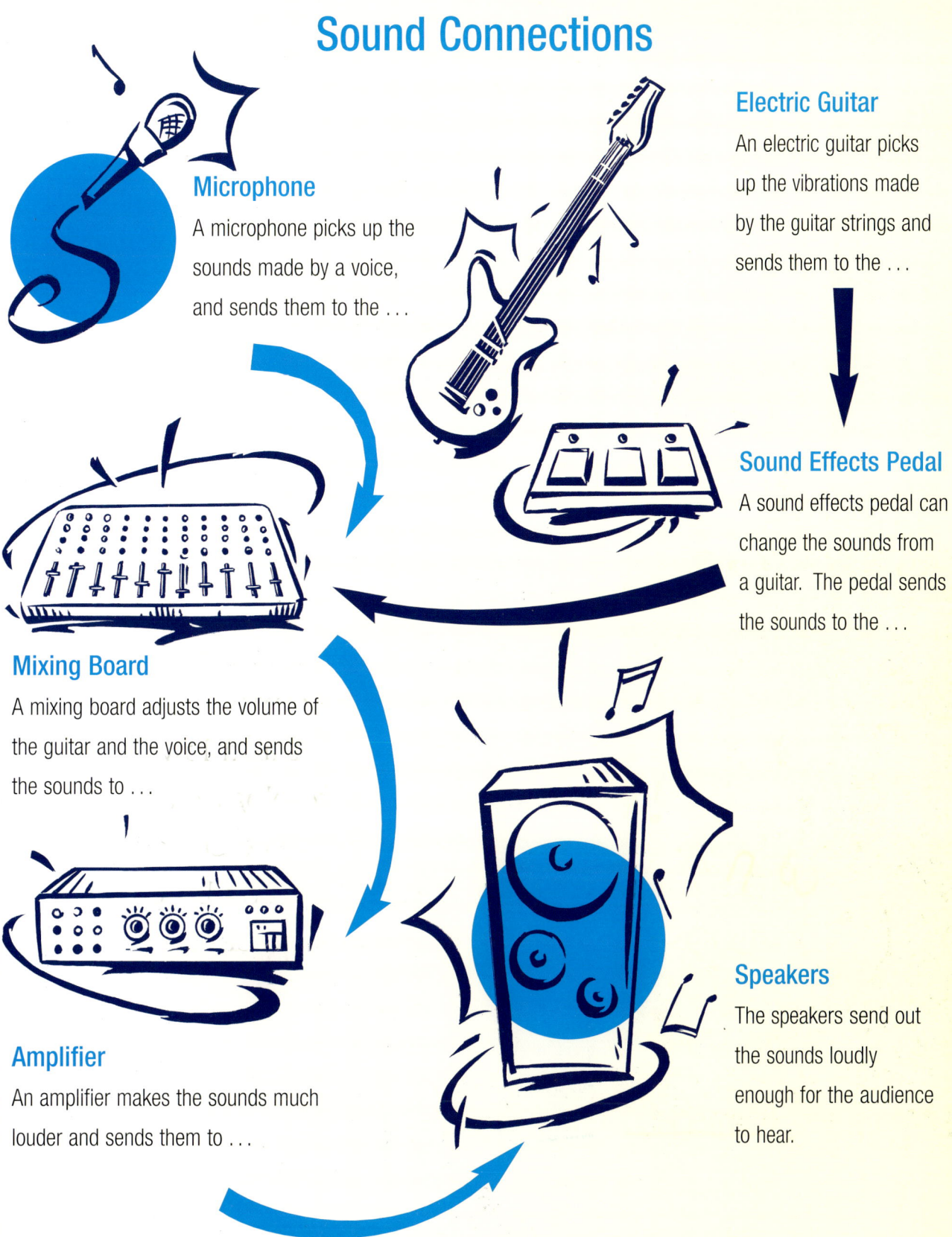

Sometimes a guitarist creates special sound effects by pressing a pedal on the stage floor. At other times, the sound crew controls the special effects from their sound console. This is called the mixing board, because the sound crew uses it to "mix" all the different instruments, voices, and special effects that create the music heard by the audience.

Special Effects

Some common special effects used in music performances are:

- **Echo:** This makes a sound like an echo bouncing back from a wall.
- **Wah-Wah:** This makes an instrument sound like a baby crying.
- **Reverb:** This makes a sound like an instrument playing in a huge room.
- **Overdrive:** This makes a fuzzy, loud, and pulsing sound.

Electric Guitars

Historians say there were instruments like guitars in ancient Egypt. During the Middle Ages they became popular in Spain and Italy. Traditional guitars have a hollow body with a hole under the strings. This hole makes the sound echo and become loud enough to hear.

During the 1950s, the electric guitar was invented in the United States. An electric guitar uses tiny magnets to pick up the vibrations of each string and convert them into electrical energy. That electrical energy is passed through wires to an amplifier, which can make very loud sounds.

6. Setting Up The Stage

When planning the concert, the lighting and the sound crews work closely together. Often the band wants certain lights to flash to the beat of their music. Or it may want to start a song with a special lighting display to get everyone really excited. Often, just as a song finishes, the lighting crew turns off all the lights for a few seconds.

Timing
Each song is carefully timed so the lighting and sound crews and the performers will know exactly when it will finish. If you look at the cover that comes with a cassette tape or a CD, you will see the times listed for each song. The times are written in minutes and seconds, so 3:53 means three minutes and 53 seconds.

If the band wants the audience to notice the lead singer or a particular band member, all the lights might go off except for a spotlight on that person. The lighting crew and the sound crew need to know the songs as well as the people performing them.

The stage has to look spectacular. The band may want stage sets specially made for the concert so that they can walk and stand on different levels to make the show look more interesting. A platform for the drums is usually built up higher than the stage floor so everyone can see the drummer behind the performing group.

Large pictures called backdrops can be painted or made and placed behind the group. Sometimes, huge video screens are placed on either side of the stage. That way, even people who are sitting a long way from the stage are able to see close-up pictures of what is happening.

Some concerts have stage sets that take days to build and cost millions of dollars.

All this building involves a lot of people working behind the scenes to have everything finished in time.

7. The Big Night

Before the night of the first concert, the band, the sound crew, the lighting crew, and other concert organizers have a rehearsal. This is a time when everyone practices to make sure that the equipment works properly and everyone knows their jobs.

If someone forgets to turn the sound on at the right time or turns the lights off at the wrong time, it can ruin the whole concert. The band practices their songs in the order that they want to perform them. The list of songs in the right order is called the playlist. The playlist is given to the lighting and sound crews so they know exactly *what* will happen and *when* it will happen.

The audience at a concert waits for a performance to begin.

Usually an hour before the show, people start arriving at the concert so they can settle into their seats early. The concert organizers sometimes hire another band to perform before the main, or headlining band. This back-up band's job is to get the audience in the right mood for the headlining band's performance.

Where is the headlining band at this point? The singers are usually warming up their voices with vocal exercises. Or they may be making sure the instruments are in tune. Some performers try to relax because they get nervous before going on stage. This nervousness is called stage fright!

Vocal Cords

We produce sounds by using our vocal cords. Our vocal cords are in our throat. They are small folds of skin that vibrate when we breathe out. This vibration makes a sound, and that sound is our voice. We use our tongue, lips, nose, and mouth to shape the sound of our voice into words.

The Three Tenors, Placido Domingo, Jose Carreras, and Luciano Pavarotti, are three of the world's most famous opera singers.

Finally, the concert is about to begin. The lighting crew turns the lights down very low. The sound crew is ready to control the music. The audience starts to cheer as it realizes that its favorite band is about to appear on stage.

Then suddenly, the lights come on in a bright blaze and music booms throughout the arena. The band is on stage, and the show has started!

8. The Show Rolls On

After the show, the band returns to its hotel to relax. However, the work hasn't finished yet. Almost immediately after the audience has left, the cleaning crew arrives to remove or recycle any trash.

> **Recycling**
>
> If the recycling symbol appears on something, it means that it can be used again. Paper, glass, and many types of plastic and metal can be collected and recycled. Recycling helps to reduce the amount of trash in our environment.

If the band has to perform in another town or country, there is no time to waste. All of the equipment, stage sets, and video screens have to be dismantled, packed, and transported by truck or airplane. The crew will be exhausted, but it has a job to do. A lot of people are anxiously awaiting the next concert.

Stage crews work hard to get everything packed up and ready for the next concert.

When everyone arrives at the next destination, all the work starts again! The trucks are unloaded, the lighting, sound, and stage equipment is set up, and rehearsals are organized—and another excited audience is entertained!

Everyone hopes it doesn't rain, that no one becomes sick, that the equipment doesn't break down, that all the tickets are sold, and that the audience loves the concert!

Index

advertising 6
ancient Egypt 4, 19
ancient Greece 4
backstage pass 5
backup band 25
compact discs 7, 20
credit card 8
electric guitar 17, 19
fax machine 9
Greece 4
light 12–13
    lighting crew 10–11, 13, 20, 21, 24, 27
mixing board 17, 18
press releases 6–7
recycling 30
rehearsal 24
seating 9
sound 15
    amplifiers 14, 15, 16, 17
    ear 15
    microphone 14, 15, 16, 17
    sound crew 14–18, 20, 21, 24, 27
    speakers 14, 16, 17
special effects 12
    echo 16, 18, 19
    filters 13
    laser lights 12
    overdrive 18
    reverb 18
    sound effects 16, 17, 18
    spotlights 12, 21
    strobe lights 12
    wah-wah 18
stage fright 26
tickets 8–9
vocal cords 26

Backstage Pass

More Bookweb books about performances!

Understudies—Fiction
A Storyteller's Journey—Nonfiction
Mystery Valley—Fiction
Face To Face—Fiction

Key To Bookweb Fact Boxes
☐ Arts
☐ Health
☐ Science
☐ Social Studies
☐ Technology

32